MW00815413

How to Start a Thrift Store Business

ISBN-13: 978-1478109594

ISBN-10: 1478109599

HOW TO START A THRIFT STORE BUSINESS

Essential Start-Up Tips to Boost Your Thrift Store Business Success

Tina Breanstor

I dedicate this book to every person – be they woman (or man) whose lives have been touched by the joy, excitement and sheer fun of shopping in a thrift store...

Contents

Thrift Store Business
An Introduction

With the sluggish economy we currently live in, it's no wonder people are turning to thrift stores more and more every day.

This has led some enterprising individuals to consider running their own thrift store operations.

Indeed, what could be a better business to run these days, with people increasingly looking for places where they can get quality products at the lowest possible prices?

If you're interested in starting your own thrift store business, then this is definitely the best time for you to do so.

However take note that many thrift shops fail simply because the proprietors weren't sufficiently prepared to run the business.

As with any business venture, planning and preparation are the keys to success in running a thrift store.

And among the first major decisions you'll need to make is whether your store will be selling strictly donated items or if you'll also be selling on consignment.

You may want to consult a business expert who can help you weigh the advantages and disadvantages of each option.

The next step would be to find the best location for your thrift shop. If possible, find an area with high foot traffic and choose the cheapest rental property in that area.

Talk to other business owners who may be able to suggest an available property. Who knows, you just might end up talking to someone who can offer you a great deal on rental property as well as one who knows how to run a thrift shop and is willing to give you some valuable advice.

Of course, you'll also need to obtain the necessary business licenses and permits, take out an insurance policy for your business, and make the necessary renovations or remodelling of the property to accommodate fixtures and retail displays.

Just because it is called a thrift store, it doesn't mean the start-up costs won't be high.

In fact, starting your own thrift store business will probably cost a lot more than you may think.

You'll have to be very patient in waiting for a significant return on your investment to show up on your financial records.

For this reason, you really must have a passion for running the business because if you're only in it for the money, then you're likely to give up before you've actually started.

Operating a thrift store will also require not just an investment in money, but also an investment in time. You can ensure the success of your business venture more effectively if you stay at the store during business hours at least for the first few months of operations.

Once the systems of operation are firmly established, you may then turn the operations over to your staff and just visit the store from time to time to oversee things.

As you probably already know, thrift stores specialize in selling used merchandise, which makes it much less expensive to start than other retail businesses.

But, just like any other business, you'll have to take some important things into consideration prior to opening your thrift shop, if you want to ensure its success.

Following is a step-by-step guide that can help you plan out your strategy for attaining business success.

Legal Aspects

1. Obtain a copy of consumer laws in your state from the department of taxation and then file a vendor's license application.

   Decide what legal structure your business is going to assume:

   -Sole proprietorship
   -LLC
   -Partnership
   -Corporation

   Decide what specific items you'll be selling in your thrift store.

If you plan on selling furniture, jewelry, beddings, or stuffed products, then check if you need a special license for those items.

2. Check area regulations for retail with your county auditor and local chamber of commerce. There may be regulations specific to your area or to the items you'll be selling in your shop. You may also need to submit an occupancy form for your store's location.

3. Check the federal regulations that apply to your thrift store business. If you plan on hiring employees, then you'll have to apply for an Employer Identification Number with the IRS so you can withhold and submit income taxes. You'll also be provided with all the necessary paperwork for you to accomplish as regards workers' compensation coverage.

Open a business bank account so you can separate your personal assets from your business assets. Set-up an accounting plan or hire an accountant to manage the financial aspect of your thrift store business.

Business Basics

1. Find the right location for your thrift shop. Consider how much storage and floor space you're going to need and then find property in a high-traffic area that can address your spatial needs. Be sure to consider the cost of renting or buying the property as well as renovation costs.

2. Obtain inventory for your thrift shop. You can get items from local auctions, garage sales, estate sales, or donations. You may also want to consider selling items on consignment.

3. Develop a marketing strategy to start building a customer base. You may hand out flyers at grocery parking lots or outside schools, malls, and churches. You may also hand out business cards at community events of post your flyers at community bulletins or other public bulletin boards.

4. Celebrate your grand opening by handing out souvenir items to the first 100 customers or offering a special opening-day discount.

It may take some time for you to see significant returns on your investment, but once your thrift store business is well-established in your area, you're sure to get a steady income stream from it.

Just be sure to keep your stocks updated and never take marketing for granted.

So now we have covered the overview let's get down to specifics.

Naming Your
Thrift Store Business

Choosing a company name can be the most fun part of starting a company. It can also be one of the most important.

After all, having the right thrift store business name can be a very effective advertising tool.

Among other things, it can give prospective customers a general idea of what your company does and what you have to offer.

In the same way, choosing the wrong name is likely to drive would-be customers away.

Here are a couple of things to remember when choosing a thrift store business name:

Keep it short and memorable

Needless to say, a short company name is much easier to remember than a lengthy one.

Choosing a short name doesn't just involve using less words, but also words with less syllables.

But, aside from being short, your thrift store business name also has to be catchy so as to promote better name recall.

You are your name

This means your company name should reflect the company's personality.

It should give people a general idea of what services you provide or what benefits they can get from patronizing your thrift store business.

You need to have an image which you want your thrift store business to project and the name you choose must fit that image.

More importantly, you have to choose a name your target customers can easily connect with.

Now, you know the basics of choosing a company name and you realize how important a name is to your business.

However, you shouldn't take the process of choosing a name too seriously.

While the company name does have to reflect its personality, it doesn't really have to define your company completely.

Take note that venturing into other related businesses is a normal part of any company's growth, so there is a real possibility that you may have to change your thrift store business name from time to time.

Again, the name of your thrift store business is important, but you shouldn't get hung up on the process of choosing it.

As long as you make sure that it's memorable, it tells people what your thrift store business is about, and you're proud of it, then you're good to go.

Drawing Up a Business Plan

Developing a new thrift store business naturally requires a good foundation, and building such a foundation begins with having a sound business plan. Remember that the business plan is an essential part of documenting a start-up business' financial goals, business objectives, and marketing plans.

Implementation of all your thrift store business ideas can only successfully begin once you've completed your business plan.

Your Business Plan: Choosing the Right Format

You probably already know that a business plan ranks among the most vital components of starting your thrift store business and ensuring its success.

But, how exactly do you make a good business plan?

Well, there are several variations and templates you can choose from. What's important is for you to choose the one that's best suited to the kind of enterprise you'll be running and to the purpose for which you're making the plan in the first place.

Here are some of the things you need to take into consideration:

1. Your Target Audience

There are two types of business plan.
a. There are business plans intended for an internal audience and these plans are usually part of your thrift store business growth strategy; they're also usually referred to as strategic plans.

b. There are also plans meant for external audiences and the purpose of these plans is usually to attract financing, suppliers, or talent for your thrift store business.

If the purpose of your business plan is primarily to get funding, then the document will typically be in condensed form, or a sort of summary of a more comprehensive business plan.

Such a version is generally known as a *funding proposal* or a *business opportunity document* and it's usually followed by the larger plan.

A business plan can indeed be a very useful document, so it's important to clearly define the audience for which it is intended.

2. What Goes Into the Plan?

Remember that a business plan needs to be comprehensive and that it's essentially created to put into writing what you envision for your thrift store business venture.

Your thrift store business plan should contain:

- An executive summary,
- The background and history of your company,
- A clear description of your thrift store business concept,
- Your marketing analysis and development plan,
- Your operations and production assessment,
- Your financial assessments and projections,
- Your human resources management assessment and plan,

- Your business implementation plan,
- An identification of resources,
- The proposed investor deal structures wherever appropriate,
- A survival strategy that describes potential risks and mitigation measures,
- Your thrift store business growth strategy,
- Your exit strategy,
- Appendices.

If that seems daunting, don't worry. Some of the components of your business plan may be longer than others and some of them are optional, depending on your target audience, the format you choose to adopt, and the purpose of your plan.

What's important is for your intended reader to clearly grasp the value proposition, understand why your thrift store business is expected to succeed, and how that success will be achieved.

If you're pitching the plan to potential investors, (or most probably the bank) then they should quickly understand your proposed deal structure and the possible returns.

3. What Length To Make Your Plan

The average business plan typically consists of 20 pages, though there are some that contain a hundred pages or more. The length of your plan will depend largely on its purpose and your target audience.

If the primary purpose of your business plan is to attract investors, then you can expect it to contain more details and therefore be lengthier than a plan that's primarily for communicating your thrift store business growth strategy.

In the same way, the business plan for a venture with a relatively simple concept should be a lot more concise than one that's made for a highly complicated enterprise.

4. Should You Use a Template or Pay a Consultant?

Many people are also confused as to whether they should hire a consultant to help them write their business plan or simply use a template for guidance. Well, it can be quite tempting to use a template or get someone else to make the plan for you. However, it's still best if you write the plan yourself even if you do decide to get some guidance from a consultant. After all, who knows your business better than you?

A solid business plan is perhaps the easiest way for you to communicate your thrift store business ideas to your target audience as well as to help you prevent problems and identify business growth strategies.

It can also be your most valuable tool when you're in search of funding for your thrift store business. Remember, though, that instead of treating it as a blueprint or a strict manual which you should implement to the letter, the plan should be seen as more of a guide in operating your thrift store business.

TIP: Even if you don't have an immediate audience for your plan, the document and even the process itself will definitely prove to be of value to your business in the long run.

Preparing a solid business plan for all the right reasons can indeed increase your chances of attaining success in your thrift store business.

How to Write the Executive Summary

The executive summary generally serves as the introduction to your formal and comprehensive business plan.

You could even say that this is Part 1 of your business plan.

It contains a summary of your thrift store business proposition, present business status, financial projections, and the key elements for success.

Although it's often tempting to just rush through this component of your business plan, always remember that an executive summary is likely to be the very first thing your target investors or banking officials will read in the document.

It basically tells the reader the status of the company currently, and where it's expected to go. Many people aren't likely to read the remainder of the plan if the executive summary doesn't catch their interest, so it's really very important to do this right.

The importance of the executive summary lies in the fact that it tells your reader exactly why you believe your thrift store business will be a success.

Brevity is the key to a solid executive summary, which generally ranges from half a page to a maximum of two pages. Writing anything longer puts you at risk of losing the reader's attention and appearing unfocused. If you can keep the summary under one page without sacrificing quality, then do so.

Note: Although it serves as the introduction, it's best to write the executive summary after you've completed your business plan. After all, it is basically a shorter version of your plan.

To keep the summary consistent with the plan itself, it should have the following components:

1. Your Mission Statement

Your business plan's executive summary is be the best place for you to express your mission statement. Make sure that statement is concise and explains in as few words as possible the existence of your thrift store business, its goals, and how you plan to achieve those goals.

In short, it should explain your thrift store business thrust to the reader. Remember to keep your mission statement focused and direct, leaving no room for confusion as regards what your thrift store business venture is all about.

2. What's Your Business Concept?

In describing your thrift store business concept, you'll need to offer some details about the kind of thrift store business you'll be running, who your target customers are, and what your competitive advantages are.

You may point out that you're filling a void you've identified in the market, offering better prices for comparable services in the industry, or offering a better service than what's currently available.

3. A Little Background

You may also want to give your reader an idea of when your venture began, who the founders are and what functions they perform, how many employees you have (or plan to hire), and where the thrift store business is located and if there are any subsidiaries or branches. A description of your offices and facilities as well as the services your offer would also be a good idea.

4. Your Thrift Store Business Status and Financial Outlook

You'll also need to give a short description of the current status of your thrift store business. Explain if your business is still in the conceptualization stage, if you've already started setting it up, or if it's already fully operational and you're simply planning to expand.

You should also mention your expected costs and your financial projections for both the short term and the long term.

This will give potential investors an idea of how much capital you need and if your business venture matches the kind of opportunity they're currently looking for. If you already have existing investors, then you'd do well to provide some information on them as well.

5. Key Factors for Success

The reader of your business plan will also appreciate getting a preview of the key factors for thrift store business success. These factors depend on your situation, of course, but it generally includes technology patents, strategic partnerships, market factors and economic trends.

If your thrift store business is already fully operational and you've had some successful projects worth noting (you may have been the first to offer a certain service in the industry), then you should include that as well.

Finally...

All in all, your business plan's executive summary should provide its reader with a quick but insightful glimpse into the plan itself.

It's advisable to highlight everything except the mission statement in bulleted lists. Include all of the important points without revealing too much, since each section is discussed in detail within the plan itself, anyway.

More importantly, make sure the summary sells the proposal on its own as much as possible, just in case reader doesn't read your plan. It does happen!

Note: It's also a good idea to draw up a table of contents right after the executive summary so the reader will know where he can find each section in the plan itself. If you're still in the process of setting up your thrift store business, then you likely won't have much to write as regards to some of the areas listed above. In that case, focus on your own experience and expertise in the field, and the circumstances that led to your thrift store business concept.

Tell your target readers how you plan to set your thrift store business apart from the competition and convince them that there's indeed a need for your business within your target niche or industry.

Company History

After the executive summary, your business plan should contain a section covering your business background or company history. The length of this portion and how it's told will depend largely on how far along your thrift store business is in terms of operations and development.

Naturally, the business history of a venture that's just starting is totally different from one that's been operating for some time. It should be about one page long, though it's understandable for a start-up company's history to cover less than an entire page.

What to Include

In this section, you should be able to illustrate how the various elements of your thrift store business venture fit together and form one successful enterprise.

You should also include some background information on the nature of the thrift store business itself and identify the factors that are expected to facilitate its success.

Furthermore, don't forget to mention the specific market needs you're planning to satisfy and the ways and methods in which you expect to satisfy these needs.

If possible, you should also identify the specific individuals or groups of people whom you believe have those needs.

An example of a specific market could be:

Mena and women aged 18 to 30 with an income of $50,000 within 50 miles of your location.

How It All Started

Among the things you should include in the company history portion of your business plan is the origin of your thrift store business concept.

This explains how you first came upon the idea for your thrift store business and why you decided to pursue that idea. You should also indicate the progress you've made so far as regards operating and growing your business venture. If you're still in the process of starting your business, then say so.

NOTE: It's also a good idea to mention the problems you've encountered along the way and how you handled each of them.

Potential investors and business partners will surely appreciate knowing that they're dealing with someone who's not afraid to deal with challenges from time to time.

Projected Short-Term Growth

You would also do well to include your short-term business growth plans in this section, so the reader will know that you've thought about your venture carefully and that you have concrete plans for its growth.

NOTE: If you're just starting a new thrift store business, then you may want to include a bit of personal history along with your background.

Among the things you can include are your educational history, technical skills, areas of expertise, relevant professional club memberships, and other thrift store businesses you may have started or companies you worked for.

TIP: You may even want to share your areas of inexperience or weaknesses and how you intend to compensate for these areas. Your target investors would definitely appreciate knowing that you're aware of the things you need to improve on and are making concrete efforts at improving them.

Finally...

In summary, the company history section of your business plan should provide an interested reader with a much better idea of how your thrift store business came to be and who you are as a businessperson.

Again, the key is to keep this section concise and avoiding unwanted information.

Organization and Management

This section of your plan includes the following:

- Your company's organizational structure

- The profiles of your management team

- Details about company ownership

- The board of director's qualifications

It's important for you to answer the question of who does what when you prepare this section.

Explain what each person's background and qualifications are. Tell your reader exactly why you've brought or are bringing these people into your organization and management team.

What exactly are they responsible and accountable for?

NOTE: You may think this section of the plan is unnecessary if you're setting up a small venture with less than five people on your team, but anybody reading your business plan needs to know who's in charge. Therefore, you should still provide a description of every department or division, along with their functions, regardless of the size of your company.

If there's an advisory board for your business, then you should also identify who's on it and how you plan to keep each member on the board.

- What salary and benefits do you plan to provide for members of your team?

- Will you be offering incentives? If so, what are they?

- How do you plan to handle promotions?

In this section of your business plan, you need to reassure your audience that the people on your team aren't going to be just names on your company letterhead.

What's Your Structure?

One very simple yet effective way of presenting your organizational structure is by creating an organizational chart and then providing a narrative description of the chart.

By doing this, you don't leave anything to chance, you're making sure the functions and responsibilities of each team member has been carefully thought out, and you've ensured that someone's in charge of each and every function in your thrift store business. Therefore, no function is taken for granted and there'll be no overlapping of responsibilities.

TIP: Remember that this kind of assurance is very important to your reader, especially if that reader is a potential investor.

Management Profiles

Ask any business expert and he'll probably tell you that among the most significant success factors in any business is the track record and ability of the management team.

This is why it's important for you to provide your reader with a background of the key members of the management team.

Specifically, you'd do well to provide resumes that indicate the name, position and the corresponding functions, primary responsibilities and level of authority, educational background, skills and experience, number of years on your team (unless it's a start-up company), compensation level and basis, previous employment and track record, industry recognitions received, and community involvement.

TIP: When you indicate the track record of your team, be sure to quantify their achievements.

For example, instead of saying:

"Extensive experience in managing a sales department"

you could say:

"Successfully managed a sales department of ten people for 15 years."

It's also a good idea to highlight how the key members of the management team complement your own experience and expertise.

If you're starting a new thrift store business, then show your reader how the unique experiences of each member of your team can contribute to your business venture's overall success.

Company Ownership

Aside from the organizational structure, this section of the plan should also describe the legal structure and provide important ownership information regarding your thrift store business.

- Has the business been incorporated? If so, then is it an S or a C corporation?

- Is your business a partnership?

- If so, then is it a limited or general partnership?

- Or are you the sole proprietor of your thrift store business?

The most important pieces of information you should include in this section are the owner/s' names, ownership percentage, form of ownership, degree of involvement of each owner within the business, common stock, and outstanding equity equivalents.

Board Qualifications

Take note that there's a huge advantage to setting up an unpaid board of advisors for your company, as it can provide you with the kind of expertise the company is otherwise unable to afford.

Simply by enlisting the help of some successful businessmen who are popular in the industry and including them in your advisory board, you'll definitely go far in enhancing the credibility of your company and encouraging a perception of expertise.

If the company has a board of directors, then you need to provide the names of the board members, their respective positions in the BOD, their background, the extent of their involvement with the thrift store business, and their expected contribution to its success.

Market Analysis

You may be a hundred percent confident about the quality of the service your thrift store business has to offer, but unless you're able to connect with your target customers, quality won't do you much good.

You'll have to get your service into your customers' hands, so to speak, to get the necessary sales. And that's why you need market analysis.

This section of your business plan should be used to illustrate your knowledge of the industry. You may also use it to present highlights and conclusions from the marketing research data you've collected.

For your analysis to be reliable, you need to study the three Cs of marketing:

1. Company

2. Customer

3. Competition

Of course, it's understandable that you should be aware of your company's strengths and weaknesses, but you should also know the same things about your competitors so you'll get a better idea of how to deal with them.

More importantly, you need to know who your customers are and what their needs and wants really are.

When you prepare the company analysis component of this section, you'll need to describe the primary industry to which your business belongs, the industry's current size and historic growth rate, the industry's characteristics and trends, and the industry's major customer groups.

All these will put into perspective the description you'll provide of the company you've established or are planning to establish.

Who Are Your Target Customers?

In choosing and defining your target customers, make sure that you narrow it down to a size that you're sure you can manage.

Many business owners make the mistake of trying to provide everything to everybody at once. Slow and sure is often a better philosophy where your business is concerned.

This section of your plan should include information that identifies the unique characteristics of your target customers including:

- Their needs

- The extent to which these needs are being met

- Demographics.

It's also a good idea to identify your target market's geographic location, who among them makes the major decisions, and any market trends that may affect your business.

The size of your target market should also be indicated in this section, along with your expected market share gains and the reason for these expected gains.
You should also indicate your pricing schedule as well as your gross margin targets and whatever discount structures you may be planning.

You'd also do well to identify what resources you plan to use to get information as regards your target market, the media you'll be using to reach the market, your target market's purchasing cycle, and the socio-economic trends likely to affect your target market.
If all this sounds complicated don't worry, just break down each section and do it one at a time.

Your Competition

Of all the Cs you need to study, your competition may be the toughest, especially if you're new to the industry. The first thing you need to do is study your direct competitors.

If you're planning to operate a thrift store business in your district, then you're likely to get direct competition from the likes of the larger multi-national thrift store businesses. So it pays to examine all the possible options on how you can set your thrift store business apart.

It's important for you to identify your direct competitors according to product or service line and market segment.

You should then assess their weaknesses and strengths, determine the level of importance of your own target market to your competitors, and identify the barriers that may pose a challenge as you enter your target niche.

This may include high investment costs, changing technology, existing patents or trademarks, customer resistance, and a difficulty in finding quality personnel.

You'd also do well to determine the market share of each key competitor and then provide an estimate of the time it'll take for new competitors to enter the niche.

Aside from looking for ways to set yourself apart from the competition, you'll also want to see how your business fits into the marketplace itself.

In doing so, you'll have to consider the strengths and weaknesses of your competitors, the possibility of competitors leaving the marketplace and new ones entering it, the services your competitors are relying on for a majority of their revenue, and effective ways of overcoming possible threats from substitute services.

Developing Your Marketing Strategy

Once all three Cs have been addressed, you should be ready to start developing your marketing program. This basically involves an analysis of what's known as the "four Ps."

They are:

1. Product,

2. Place,

3. Price,

4. Promotion.

Product, of course, refers to what you plan to sell (in this case your thrift store service)

Place refers to where you plan to sell it (office, online, or both).

Price refers to the amount you'll charge for each service you'll be offering.

And Promotion refers to the incentives and other promotional strategies you plan to use in order to get your target market to try your services.

To put it simply, a marketing strategy is your way of drawing in customers, which is indeed very important since customers are essentially the lifeblood of any business venture.

There isn't a single way of approaching a marketing strategy. What's important is for your strategy to be uniquely applicable to your thrift store business and part of a continuing evaluation process that aims to facilitate business growth and success.

In conducting a "four Ps" analysis, you'll likely conduct some market tests and you'd do well to include the results of these tests in this section of your business plan. All other details of the tests may be attached as an appendix.

The information you provide in this section may include the number of customers who participated in the tests, demonstrations or any information provided to the participating customers, the degree of importance of satisfying the needs of your target market, and the percentage of participants who expressed desire to take advantage of your products and/or services.

After creating your marketing strategy, you'll also need to draw up a sales strategy, which outlines the methods you'll be using to actually sell the services you plan to offer.

There are two very important elements of a good sales strategy.

- The first is your sales force strategy, which determines if you'll be employing internal sales personnel or independent representatives.

  You should also identify the number of people you plan to recruit for your company's sales force as well as the recruitment and training strategies you'll be using.

You'd also do well to present the compensation packages you've lined up for your sales personnel.

- The second element of a sales strategy is a description of the sales activities you've lined up for the company.

A sales strategy is made more manageable when broken down into activities.

For example, you could start with identifying prospective customers and then prioritizing your prospects according to those who have the highest potential of buying your products.

From this outline of activities, you can easily determine the number of prospects you may have to get to make a sale and the average amount you'll likely earn from each sale.

You'll also need to draw up a solid market development plan in order to make your market analysis work to your advantage. While the information in your development plan is likely to come into play only when your company has been established and operational for at least a few years, potential investors will surely appreciate the fact that you've already envisioned your company's growth and evolution.

Among other things, your development plan should provide answers to the following questions:

- ➢ Is the market for the services you offer currently growing?

- ➢ Are you planning to offer line extensions or new services within your first few years of operations?

- ➢ Does the market development plan you've crafted offer ways of increasing the overall demand for your services within the industry?

- ➢ Are there alternative ways of making your company more competitive?

Remember that the market analysis is a vital part of your business plan and it's likely to take up a large part of the plan itself. This is why it's necessary to conduct a thorough research on the competition and on the market you're planning to enter.

Finally…

You may have the best service in the market, but without an organized and well-crafted market analysis and development plan, you still won't be able to guarantee success. You market analysis helps you identify a clear roadmap of how to bring your services to your target customers.

Financial Projections

Making financial projections for a start-up thrift store business can be described as both science and art.

Investors may want to see you spell out financial forecasts in cold, hard numbers, but it's not really that easy to predict the financial performance of your thrift store business several years from now, especially if you're still in the process of raising capital.

Simply put, this is the part where you formally request funding from potential investors and you do that by illustrating how much funding you need for start-up as well as within the first five years of operations. If you already have an existing business and are looking towards expansion, then you may reflect the funding requirements for the expansion itself.

Potential investors are also sure to appreciate some historical data as regards the financial performance of your company, particularly within the last three years or so, depending on how long you've been in business. If you have any collateral that can possibly be used to secure a loan, then that's worth noting as well.

Difficulty aside, financial projections are requirements for a solid business plan and you'll really have to deal with them if you truly want to catch your prospective investors' attention.

Regardless of whether your business is a start-up or a growing venture, you'll still need to provide historical and/or projected financial data.

Here are a few useful tips:

1. **Don't let spreadsheets intimidate you**

All financial projections necessarily start with spreadsheet software, with Microsoft Excel being the most commonly used; chances are great you already have the software on your computer.

Other than this, there are also some special software packages that can help you with financial projections. These packages often provide flexibility, which allows you to weigh alternate scenarios or change assumptions quickly whenever necessary.

2. Create short-term projections as well as medium-term projections

Specifically, your prospective investors should see financial projections for the first year of operations, broken down into monthly projections. You should also provide a three-year financial projection that's broken down into yearly projections and a five-year financial projection. It's advisable, however, to keep your five-year projection separate from your business plan, but readily available in case a potential investor asks to see it. When you project business growth, be sure to consider the current state of your market, trends in labour and costs, and the possibility of needing additional funding for future expansion.

3. Make sure start-up fees are accounted for

Never forget to include fees for permits, licenses, and equipment in your short-term projections. You should also keep the difference between variable and fixed costs in mind when making your projections and differentiate between the two wherever necessary. Variable costs are usually placed under the "costs for goods sold" category.

4. **Go beyond your income statement**

While your income statement is the basic measuring tool by which projected expenses and revenue can be conveyed, a solid financial projection will go beyond that to include projected balance sheets that show a breakdown of your assets, liabilities, and equity, among other things.

You'd also do well to include cash flow projections that reveal cash movement through the company within a given period.

Estimates of the amount you plan on borrowing as well as expected interest payments on those loans should also be included.

Furthermore, you should make sure your financial projections are all in accordance to the GAAP.
TIP: If you're new to financial reporting or don't understand the last paragraph, then you may want to consider hiring an accountant to review your projections.

5. **Offer two scenarios only**

Although you need to go beyond the simple income statement, remember that where financial projections are concerned, potential investors really want to see only two scenarios: The best- and worst-case scenarios. Anything more than those two are superfluous and may just cause unnecessary confusion, so skip it.

Finally...

To sum up, this section should tell potential investors how much money you need now and in the near future, your preferred type of funding and terms, and how you intend to use the funds.

NOTE: Take note that the intended use of the funds is a vital piece of information for potential investors and would-be creditors, which is why you need to explain it in this section.
It's also important to include all pertinent business-related information that can possibly affect the future financial situation of your company. A trend analysis for your financial statements is also very helpful, especially if you present it with graphs, as this is easier to see.

TIP: Above all, you should strive to make reasonable and clear assumptions.

As previously mentioned, financial forecasting is both a science and an art. You'll need to make several assumptions, but you'll also have to be realistic when making those assumptions. Going overboard will likely raise red flags for potential investors, so always make sure your projections are backed up by solid research.

Calculating Your Start-up Costs

What are start-up costs?

These are the expenses you have to deal with before your new thrift store business can actually begin operations and earn revenue.

The concept of start-up costs is very important in tax law because these costs are not considered as deductible expenses, unlike most of the other business costs. You will, instead, need to amortize these costs over the course of a few months or years.

This means you'll only be able to deduct part of the start-up costs each year.

And you can only determine and take full deduction on your other expenses after you have determined start-up costs.

The first step

The first step in calculating the start-up costs of your business is to gather all of the expense receipts from business-related transactions.

Next, determine the exact date when your thrift store business opened and then separate the receipts into two piles: one pile for the expenses from before your business opened and another pile for expenses incurred after the opening day.

The next step is to remove all of the receipts for items such as research costs, taxes, and deductible interest from the pile receipts before opening day.
These costs can immediately be deducted.

Finally, add together all the remaining receipts belonging to your "before opening date" pile. The sum is your total start-up costs, which have to be amortized.

Amortization is usually set over a period of 18 months, and expenses like hiring and training costs, pre-opening advertising, and travel expenses to meet potential suppliers are usually included in the amortized start-up costs.

How to Obtain Business Grants

When starting a business there can be some huge barriers standing in your way, among the biggest of which are start-up costs and other business-related expenses.

You may be planning to take out a loan for the purpose of starting your thrift store business.

Why don't you consider applying for grants from the government or from private organizations instead? There are several reasons why grants are better than a loan, the most obvious of which is the fact that grants don't need to be repaid.

How exactly can you obtain a business grant and turn your simple idea into a thriving thrift store business?

The Catalog of Federal Domestic Assistance is a good place for you to search for a specific grant you can apply for because it contains a list of all grants available for small thrift store businesses.

The catalog also indicates what type of business qualifies for a particular grant, so you can immediately determine which grants your thrift store business is likely to qualify for.

Another option is for you to visit the Small Business Administration's website, which promotes federal grant programs that offer almost $2 billion to small businesses, particularly those focusing on providing technological solutions to existing business issues.

Once you have identified the grant programs you will be applying for, you should start preparing a business plan.

Take note that grant organizations base their approval or rejection of your application on the contents of your thrift store business plan.

- Your plan should therefore include a statement of purpose that is clearly written and effectively defines the goals of your company.

- A good thrift store business description, an outline of your short-term and long-term goals, a discussion on planned marketing strategies, and a projected financial analysis should also be part of your plan.

The financial section of your plan is very important because organizations usually measure the worth of a candidate based on how you plan to use the grant money.

You should therefore make sure that your financial analysis and hypothetical budget are both conservative and realistic.

When your thrift store business plan is complete, it's time to create your actual grant proposal.

If you have previous experience in creating such a proposal, then you can save some money by writing the proposal yourself.

However, if you've never written a grant proposal before, then it would be wise to hire the services of a professional writer.

Make sure your proposal includes schematics, reports, and some basic information on planned projects that are likely to be influenced by the grant funds.

Furthermore, grant reviewers are likely to appreciate such attention to detail, which may be seen as a strong commitment to your product.

In this case, the reviewers will be more likely to approve your applying for grant funds. Complete your grant application by including an updated list of contacts. This list should start with the contact details of the top-level employees.

It should also include the contact details of individuals who can provide important details on the supplementary materials included in your application. Make sure that all pertinent information on your thrift store business and requested files by the grant organization are included in your application.

If your application lacks any of these files, then the grant is likely to be denied or the processing could be very slow. Submit your application only when you're sure that it's complete.

It's also a good idea to have your grant application reviewed by family, friends, and colleagues so grammatical errors can be cleared up and anything you may have overlooked can be pointed out to you. And as a final review process, you should schedule a reading session together with your staff, so you can correct any identified problems.

Above all, you should be patient.

Take note that the process of getting approved for grants may take longer to complete than the process of getting approved for loans.

This is because grant applications are reviewed a number of times and most grant organizations have to go through thousands of applications at a time.

Building Inventory

Of course, your thrift store can't possibly open unless you fill your shelves with inventory first.

The first decision you need to make in this regard is what kind of items you want to deal with.

When it comes to quantity, it's best to take the middle of the road. Your inventory should be sizable enough for shoppers to find interesting, but still small enough to encourage a quick turnover.

For starters, you may collect inventory from relatives, friends, and colleagues, and then build it up gradually. You could also ask businesses to donate items or cash for your thrift store.

The cash donation will go a long way towards helping you open and operate your store, and the donated goods don't even have to be items you can sell. Rather, you could ask material donations like shelves, tables, chairs, and counters, among other things. Local businesses generally have a lot of stuff they no longer use, but still keep in their storage area and they're likely to give you the support you need.

You may be surprised there are usually a lot of people out there who want to join in and help out with this kind of project. All you have to do is ask.

Family, friends, and neighbours can donate clothing and other items they no longer need, but which can still be of use to others. Old furniture that is still in good condition can be extremely valuable and is great for making your store look homely and welcoming.

As a retailer, you should try to be selective about choosing your merchandise so as to provide your customers with compelling products as well as a presentation that allows you to maximise sales and promotes quick inventory turnover.

That is what you call classic retail merchandising. In a perfect world the perfect balance is struck and every item on sale is presented in its best angle.

A properly run thrift store is typically an ever-changing treasure trove of items that appeal to everyone. Merchandised imaginatively and successfully you can create a warm and inviting ambience.

Because every item in your shop is one-of-a-kind and because the items are priced for quick turnover, you are effectively able to convey a sense of urgency (buy now or miss out on this one-of-a-kind item) to your target customers. However you need to be selective about the items you sell, regardless of whether they're donated, found or bought from garage sales.

It's important for you to establish a reputation for selling stylish items of good quality so your customers are assured of getting good value for their money.

Make sure each item you sell isn't in need of repair and be sure to clean your merchandise before displaying it on your shelves. If you create the atmosphere of an upscale boutique in your thrift store, then people are likely to see it that way and therefore respect the prices you charge for your items.

Just about anything people in your community can donate will help you turn your store into a successful venture. You may also ask for help in making flyers and posters announcing the opening of your thrift store.

There are many people who are well-off, but prefer buying items in thrift shops rather than paying over-the-top prices for new mass-produced goods. Thrift stores aren't really just for the underprivileged, but for people who want to help the community while getting great bargains.

Theme Your Thrift Store

Ask yourself what kinds of products you're naturally interested in and what particular types of customers you want to target, and then use that as the theme for your shop. Be careful not to try to sell just any type of goods you lay your hands on, or your shop will be just like any other store in your area.

Set yourself apart by being known for themes like 1950's clothing, retro evening wear, vintage crafts or any theme that lends itself to the thrift store look, and then source your goods based on those themes.

You may also want to theme sections of your store by color. The big retailers do this all the time. Pick one color and gather together related items to form an eye-catching display.

This is great for encouraging customer to buy into your products as they can see how they all match and go together.

Of course, you should also make sure the name of your business, your logo, your business cards, and all your advertising materials make it easy for potential customers to understand what your theme is.

Setting Your Prices

Pricing is another all-important consideration when setting up. Just because your merchandise is pre-owned doesn't mean you have to price it too low.

The standard rule is to set a price that's about 25%-40% of the original price. While you don't need to price your items too low, you should also refrain from pricing them too high, as that can cause them to remain unsold for months. You also need to decide at the outset what price your willing to pay for stock. A quarter of the retail price is generally accepted.

Creating Systems and Procedures

Once your store has been organised, it's also important to establish operational procedures right from the start. You need to maintain accounts and keep track of your stock coming in. You'll also need an appropriate system for handling obsolete and unsold stock.

Getting Insurance for Your Thrift Store Business

So, you have an idea for a good thrift store business venture; you even have the name for your new thrift store business already.

And you've also proceeded to create a business plan and a proposal for a grant application.

What else do you need to do prior to actually operating your thrift store business?

You will need good insurance.

This is actually one of the most important steps you need to take when starting a thrift store business. The good news is that there are lots of great places where you can get good advice on the different types of insurance that you may need for your new thrift store business.

An insurance agent is probably the best person for you to approach if you're looking for advice on getting insurance for your thrift store business.

More specifically, you should hire the services of an agent for an insurance company that specializes on thrift store business insurance rather than a general insurance company.

You have to understand that you'll be dealing with a totally different set of risks and challenges with a business than you would with a car or with your home. Getting insurance from a company that specializes in thrift store business insurance assures you that the agent you're dealing with really knows what he's talking about.

You can expect the insurance agent to lay out several different insurance options for you.

These options can range from liability insurance for your thrift store business to auto insurance.

You may also be offered property insurance as well as loss of business coverage, which protects your interests in case a fire breaks out and you end up without a business to run for a month or so.

It's important for you to ask questions and make sure you understand what each type of insurance covers you for so you can be sure to make an informed decision as to which types of insurance you're going to get. More often than not, you'll be presented with more insurance options than you can afford.

There's also a possibility that the insurance agent you're consulting will present you with more insurance options than your business actually needs. This makes it even more important for you to understand what each type of insurance covers.

Furthermore, the start of a business is usually a time when you will have to take a few risks by taking out less insurance than your thrift store business needs.

You'll have to decide how much you can afford to spend for insurance and which type of insurance is the most needed by your thrift store business.

Once you've determined this, you can leave the other types of insurance for later.

Most thrift store businesses start only with loss of business coverage, others with liability insurance.

The point is to get only the most important insurance coverage that you can afford for starters. As your company grows, it will become more important for you to protect your thrift store business' assets.
And the good news is that you may able to afford it at that time.

Aside from the insurance that you have previously identified as a need for your thrift store business, there may also be other types of insurance that your customers expect you to have.

You can work on getting these additional insurance types when the right time comes.

How to Trademark Your Thrift Store Business Name and Logo

If you have just put up a new thrift store business, you should be careful not to stop at choosing a name and logo for it.

You should also make sure that the name and logo you chose is adequately protected.

This is especially important if one of your business goals is to create an instantly recognizable brand. The best way to protect your business name and logo is to have it trademarked.

Take note that a trademark is also used to protect symbols, drawings, and any other character associated with your thrift store business, much like a patent protects inventions.

The whole process of getting your business name and logo trademarked is a relatively simple one.

However, it often takes several months for your trademark registration to really become official.

Following is a quick guide on how you can protect your business name and logo by getting it trademarked.

1. Choose the name and design the logo for your new thrift store business.

   You have to make sure, of course, that the name and logo you choose are not yet being used by any other company.

   More importantly, you need to ensure that such name and logo have not already been trademarked by someone else.

You can check the database of the official trademark office to make sure you won't run into any legal problems with your chosen name and logo.

2. Once you have established that your chosen thrift store business name and logo are not yet trademarked, request for and fill-out the necessary paperwork.

   Once the paperwork has been filled out and submitted to the Patent and Trademark Office, the processing of your application for registration will officially begin.

3. Allow five months for the processing to be completed.

   If five months have passed and you still have not received any notification of your trademark having been filed, you may check on its status. Take note, though, that it usually takes between five and seven months for a trademark registration process to be completed.

4. Once you receive notification of your trademark having been filed, obtain a copy of it from the trademark office.

   Take note that you will be asked for your registration number when you make the request for a copy of your trademark certificate.

5. Between the fifth and sixth year of your trademark registration, make sure that an

"Affidavit of Use" is filed, so as to prevent other companies from using your trademarked name and logo.

You should remember to file two other affidavits as well before every 10-year period of owning the trademark has passed.

Writing an
LLC Operating Agreement

Limited Liability Corporation, or LLC, is the ideal set-up for start-up companies and small businesses because it requires the business owner to take on only limited liability for the company.

And the good news is that creating an LLC is fairly simple and inexpensive. Take note that the operations of an LLC are governed by the LLC operating agreement.

You'll therefore need to learn how to write your LLC operating agreement.

Here is a step-by-step guide:

1. Gather basic information such as the company name and location as well as the names and physical addresses of the members of your company. You should also note your agent's name.

2. Gather all financial information. This includes each member's initial contribution to the company and how much each of them will own in terms of percentage of company interest. You can choose to have either a single-member or multi-member LLC.

   For example, you could choose to initially make a contribution of $100 and own a hundred percent of the company.

   What's important is for all company members to be included in your LLC operating agreement.

3. Choose and download a sample agreement.

   Of course, you can choose to write your own agreement from scratch, but working from a sample would definitely make the process much easier for you.

   While operating agreements aren't really that complex, the language used can be very governmental, and basing your agreement on a sample will help ensure that the language is interpreted correctly.

4. Determine if you need the services of a registered agent.

   Take note that there's a slight difference in the LLC laws of each state.

   The operating agreement typically has a space that needs to be filled in for the registered agent. If your state's requirements allow it, you can be the one to fill in this space.

5. Check the "Business Purpose" section of your sample agreement and make sure it includes the statement that indicates your company's purpose as engaging in lawful acts or activities for which an LLC may be formed.

   You should also check the language in the "Term" section. "Indefinitely" is commonly used for the term.
   In the terms of dissolution, "by a majority" is also commonly used.

6. You should also check the language in the "Management" section.

   A majority of small thrift store businesses are managed by the members as a whole, but you also have the option of getting managers for your thrift store business, especially if there are active and passive members.

   Whatever you decide, make sure your agreement contains the appropriate language as to how your company will operate.

7. Personalize the sample agreement by inserting the data from the notes you took as per Step 1 and Step 2. Be sure to include the necessary signature lines.

8. Print the agreement as well as a list of all members with their respective addresses and then staple them together.

   Let all members sign the agreement, have it photocopied, and then provide each member with a copy.

   Be sure to keep the original somewhere safe and have additional copies in your files for reference.

Take note that this step-by-step guide does not constitute legal advice.
If there's anything about forming an LLC that you don't understand, it's still best to seek the advice of an attorney.

Writing a Company Brochure

A company brochure, also known as a corporate brochure, is an excellent way of introducing your thrift store business to your target market.

That is, of course, if you do it right.

The very first things you need to take into consideration are the logo, font, and color you use on your brochure.

People will only learn about your thrift store business if they read the brochure, and they are more likely to read a brochure if the cover has an attractive design, which is why your choice of logo, font, and color is very important.

Take note as well that people are more likely to patronize your thrift store business if you're able to build a connection with them and if you're able to establish in their minds the thought that you can be trusted.

The best way to do this using a brochure is to include pertinent information such as the background and history of your company, what you have to offer, and how you intend to deliver whatever it is you're offering. You may also include information on how your company intends to serve the community as a whole.

Furthermore, you'll need to provide an explanation of what the brochure itself is all about.

- Is it just about the organization or does it present the products and services as well?

- Is it all about the industry and what role your company plays in its development?

- Is it for a specific event where your company is a participant or is it a detailed brochure of your company?

And of course, you'll have to tell the reader at the outset what the brochure's relevance to him is.

Therefore, before you even start writing your company brochure, you'll first have to think about what you want the brochure to portray and who your target audience is.

You may want to set-up a brainstorming session with your company's key personnel for this purpose.
And take note that even as your brochure contains all the necessary information as discussed above, it should remain concise and easy to read.

You should also make it easy for the reader to select which particular piece of information he wants to read. This can be achieved through the use of headings and sub-titles.

As long as you keep these tips in mind, you should be able to create a company brochure that truly presents your thrift store business in a positive light.

Leasing Space

Having enough space for your business is one of the most critical factors in operating your new business. In choosing retail sales space, you'll have to take several things into consideration.

Among these things are good visibility of the location from the street, and easy access for your customers. You'll also have to decide if you're going to build, buy, or rent your retail sales space.

There are many advantages to renting space as opposed to buying or building.

Maintenance, flexibility, and taxes are perhaps the three most important advantages.

Maintenance

If you rent retail sales space, you'll be responsible only for a bit of routine maintenance issues like the replacement of light bulbs, repairing uninsured damages caused by negligence on your part, and cleaning the premises.

The good news for you is that major maintenance issues like electrical, plumbing, air conditioning, heating, and structural problems are the responsibility of your landlord.

This means that if your roof starts to leak, it will be your landlord's responsibility to have it repaired. Knowing that your rent already covers major maintenance issues makes it so much easier for you to budget your company's available funds.

Flexibility

Renting space helps you avoid being forced to stay at the same location even when it's no longer practical to do so.

Even if you have a lease contract for a specific period, that's still a lot better than getting locked into a commercial mortgage.

If the demographics in your area change, then it will be much easier to relocate your thrift store business if you're simply leasing or renting space.

This also holds true for the time when your thrift store business has grown such that you need more space. Furthermore, you won't have to worry about selling your existing location if you have to move to a new place, which is an issue you'll have to deal with if you own the space.

Taxes

It's very easy to understand the advantages of renting space where taxes are concerned.

Rental payments are considered business expenses and are therefore deductible.

On the other hand, only the interest that you pay for commercial mortgages is deductible.

You have to consider as well, the fact that commercial property often doesn't appreciate as much as residential properties, which means your property may accrue very little equity over time.

When you weight this against the 100% deductibility of commercial rent, you'll realize how advantageous it is to simply lease retail space.

Now that you understand the benefits of leasing retail sales space, you'll have to learn how to find the perfect location for your thrift store business.

Remember that leasing will affect not only your company's profit, but also its ability to grow as well as the satisfaction level of your employees.

So, before you go out looking for space to rent, you'll have to know exactly what you are looking for.

Here's how to identify the perfect retail sales space for your thrift store business:

1. Determine how much space your thrift store business needs now and how much it may need in the future. The rule of thumb in determining space requirements is to have 175-250 sq. ft. of space for each person who will be working at the location.

2. Contact a real estate agent and seek advice in finding a suitable commercial space.

    Agents typically have the inside scoop on what'd going on in the real estate market and they can advise you properly on which particular properties are ideal for your purposes.

    It's a good idea to contact a real estate firm that specializes in office space rentals.

3. Discuss any necessary improvements with your potential landlord. Take note that improvements are usually subject to serious negotiations, especially if there are lots of vacancies. You would also do well to check out the parking space. Does the rental offer a number of slots you can set aside for yourself and your employees, or would you have to compete with the public for street parking?

4. You may be able to reduce rental cost by either sharing space or looking out for incubators. You could share your reception area, rest rooms, and conference rooms with another small firm to reduce your rental costs – that is, if you're okay with having less privacy.

   Incubators are small unused areas in a larger building which are usually offered for lease at much lower costs.
   These are also good options for a small thrift store business like yours, provided it meets with your requirements, of course.

5. You may also want to consider renting an all-inclusive suite. The rate for executive office suites is usually higher, but they usually come fully-furnished and provide you with access to meeting rooms and office equipment, thus significantly reducing your up-front costs. Many of these suites even come with a receptionist.

6. Before signing a lease contract, be sure to review it exhaustively.

Check the indicated monthly payment, how long the lease is for, what maintenance and repair concerns the landlord will be responsible for, and things like annual rent increases in accordance with inflation.

You'd also do well to check if there are provisions concerning the possibility of terminating the lease early as well as provisions regarding internet connections, cable service, telephone lines, and other company needs. Other important details for you to review include the date of occupancy, right of refusal for the adjoining space, security, and other amenities.

7. Finally, it's a good idea for you to hire a qualified real estate attorney. Make sure the attorney specializes in negotiations for leases and that he knows your area. It's a bonus if he has dealt with the same kind of thrift store business in the past. This is important because lease negotiations typically cover hundreds of terms, which makes it a definite advantage to have someone who's gone through it all before on your side.

Managing Your Employees

Once you have your new thrift store business in place, you'll have to deal with managing your employees, which can be a very tricky process.

If you're not careful, you just might end up babysitting rather than running a successful thrift store business venture.

This is especially true if a majority of your employees are paid very low hourly rates.

You're lucky if you can hire wonderful employees who don't give you any problems.

However, you'll still have to find effective ways of keeping these wonderful employees in your thrift store business, and that's where good employee management comes in.

Perhaps the most important aspect of employee management is your ability to set very clear goals and communicate your company objectives very clearly to your employees.

Take note that goal-setting and communicating objectives have to be done regularly.

The more you communicate with your employees in an honest and open manner, the easier it will be for you to manage them. It's advisable to set monthly, quarterly, and annual goals. And you have to make sure the goals you set are mutual.

This means you should not be forcing your employees to work towards your own goals.

The employees themselves have to believe in those goals and they'll have to be taught how to adjust in case circumstances that keep them from attaining those goals suddenly arise.

Furthermore, you need to realize that goals don't really mean much unless employees' compensations are largely tied up with those goals. The compensation may be in the form of bonuses, commissions, or salary percentages.

What's important is for the employees to have a good motivation for working towards the company's goals. It's also a good idea to hold a yearly meeting with all of your employees where an annual review will be conducted.

During this review, you should commend your employees for the things they're doing right and discuss solutions for the things that didn't quite work out. Identifying areas of improvement and finding solutions together can give employees the assurance that they really are part of the company and that they're being valued as individuals, not just as paid workers.

Finally, another very important part of employee management is getting feedback on how YOU are doing at your job.

- How are you as a manager?

- What are you doing right?

- What else can you do to become a better manager?

You have to realize that getting feedback from your employees isn't a waste of your time.

Quite the contrary, in fact.

More often than not, the best ideas for improving a thrift store business come from the front-liners, as they're usually the ones who know exactly what the customers want.

How to Market Your
Thrift Store Business

Marketing your new thrift store business probably ranks among the most challenging aspects of putting up a business venture, not to mention that it can also be the most fun.

You should, in fact, be excited about marketing your thrift store business.

- The main purpose of marketing a thrift store business is to let your target customers know that you exist and that you have a lot of benefits to offer them.

And take note that the kind of message you convey to your target market is crucial when you market a new thrift store business.

Even if you're selling exactly the same item as your closest competitor, you're more likely to come out on top of the competition if you're able to come up with better marketing strategies and if you can successfully create a brand for your company.

Creating a brand for your company will make your thrift store business more valuable to potential customers.

Regardless of what type of business you're into branding is still important.

In fact, the more you create an attractive personality around your company brand, the more you set yourself apart from the competition, thus giving your thrift store business a much better opportunity for growth.

How do you know your brand is effective?

Simple.

Market it to yourself.

Imagine that you're a would-be customer taking stock of a new player in the industry.

- Does the company brand look, sound, and feel authentic?

- Is it a fun and attractive brand?

Remember that marketing your thrift store business has to be fun, so don't take it too seriously.

And even while you're working hard to create a brand, you should always remain true to yourself.

That is what will make your brand truly authentic. And an authentic brand is something your competition can never take away.

In conclusion...

Establishing a thrift store in your locality is something just about anyone can do given a bit of time and careful preparation.

You, too, can start your own thrift store business with a little help from other people in your community, particularly from your family and friends.

You can opt to start your thrift store with just one type of item or offer a variety of items carrying the same or similar theme.

Keep the quality high at all times.

Price your items reasonably and change your merchandise often to keep a fresh look. Re-invent your store regularly to ensure that it not only thrives, but prospers with time.

The good thing about a thrift store is that it's the kind of business that can benefit not just the store owner, but the entire community and it can even be of significant help to people in need.

It's definitely a great business idea that can make a difference in many people's lives.

Good luck.

Made in the USA
Middletown, DE
29 August 2020